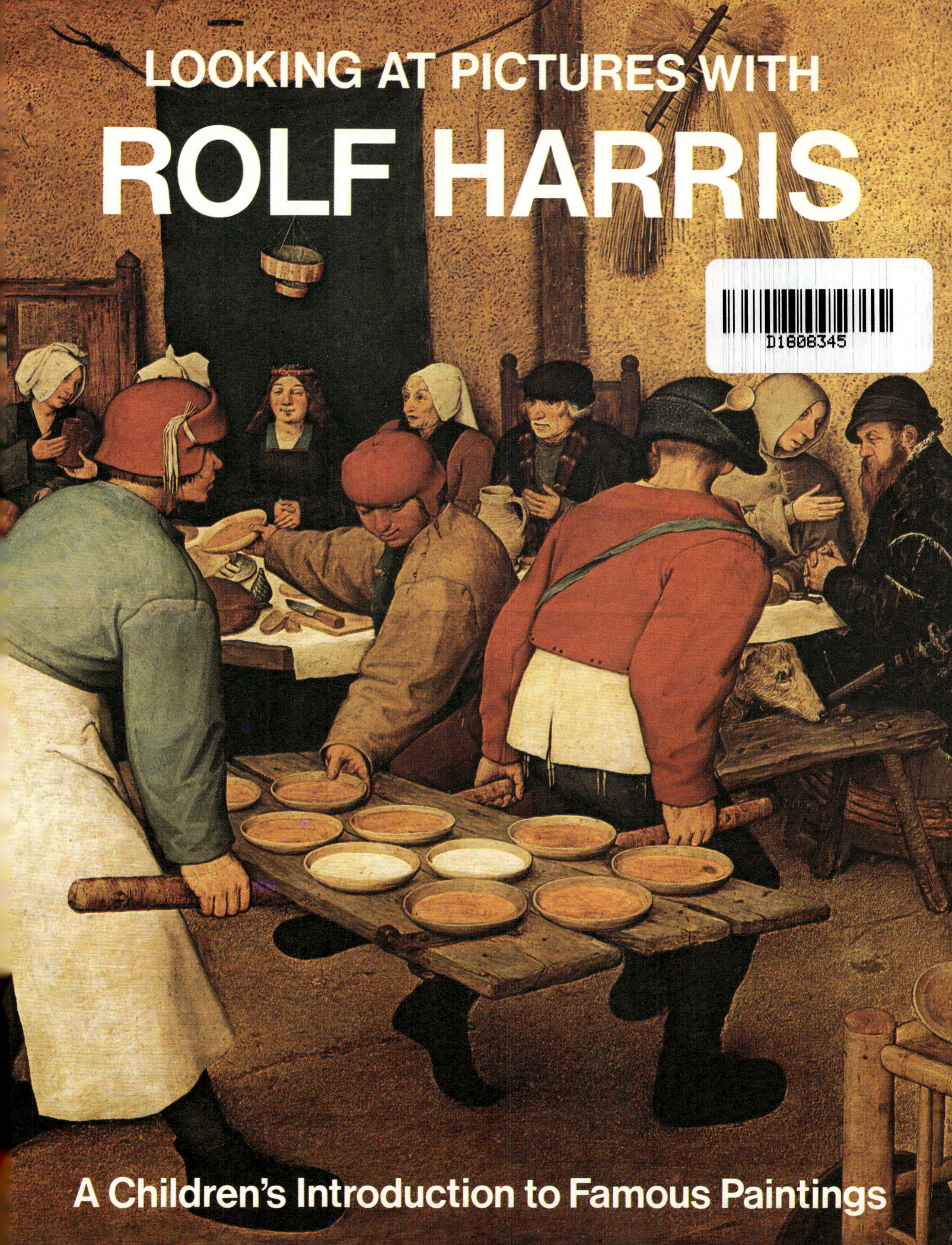

LOOKING AT PICTURES WITH
ROLF HARRIS

A Children's Introduction to Famous Paintings

List of illustrations

OPPOSITE Sharaku (active 1794–5), *Actors Ichikawa Omezo and Otani Oniji II* (detail). 1794. 14 × 9½ in. London, British Museum.

PICTURES ARE FUN!

Pictures are fun. Just think what a painter can do. He can take you instantly to any country in the world, or to a place that has never existed —except in his imagination. What's more, he can drop you there today, a hundred years in the future or a thousand years in the past. A good painting, if you give it the chance, can whirl you off into another day and age in a flash. It can make you happy or sad. Isn't that exciting?

As a youngster I loved looking through the old art catalogues my father had. They opened up new worlds for me, and I can remember some of them vividly to this day. One, called *The Source*, was a portrait of a beautiful redheaded girl in some strange dark cavern. What did it mean? I used to conjure up all sorts of stories around that mysterious face. Another picture I recall in every detail showed a row of poplars across a meadow and a stream—the first oil painting I ever tried myself was a copy of this English country scene.

I could go on and on about the pictures that spring to mind. There's *The Laughing Cavalier* (by Franz Hals), which I love to this day. Apart from showing you the sort of clothes a man wore in those far-off days, the artist magically makes you smile and almost laugh at some amusing confidence which seems to be shared between just the two of you. It's good to be able to see in paintings how folks once lived and worked, even to see the games the children were playing. And it's easy to identify with them.

Please have fun with this book. A good painting never goes stale—and the deeper you go into it the more you get out of it. So hop into it! It's good!

Phaidon Press Ltd, Littlegate Ho., St Ebbe's St, Oxford. First published 1978.
ISBN 0 7148 1857 7. Printed in Great Britain by Morrison & Gibb Ltd, London and Edinburgh.

Introduction

Pictures by thirty-five artists

There are forty-six pictures to look at in this book, drawn or painted by thirty-five artists from all over the world. Some of them are alive today, some died many hundreds of years ago, but they have all left pictures for us to enjoy—pictures which show how they saw the world they lived in. You can't expect to like them all, but there will probably be several which appeal to you straight away, and others which you will return to later. The pictures are grouped under different headings, such as 'Animals' and 'Faces'. This is partly so you can turn to a subject which interests you, but also so that you can compare how different artists have treated a similar subject.

Making comparisons

When you compare pictures it helps to find out from the caption when each artist lived and where. A date on its own might not mean much, but it's more interesting, for example, to compare Van Gogh's paintings (pages 8–11) with Renoir's (p. 35) when you realise that they were both painting in France at about the same time (and even had some friends in common). A painting is often a fascinating 'window on the past', showing exactly how people lived in a period when there were no cameras to record them. In fact, the more you know about a painting, the more interesting it becomes. For instance, Richard Dadd's *The Fairy Feller's Master-Stroke* (p. 27) is weird and wonderful in itself, but far creepier when you know that he was quite mad when he painted it!

Looking ahead

When you want to see other pictures by an artist you like, you will have to find more books or visit an art gallery. It can be very exciting to see the original of a favourite painting in an exhibition, and it nearly always looks a little bit different from the reproduction. Sometimes it seems unexpectedly small, and sometimes too far away for all the detail to be visible, but it is always worthwhile going to have a look if you get the chance.

The Picture

This is the sort of picture that almost everybody likes (you've probably seen it on Christmas cards). There's plenty to look at, it's beautifully painted, and the colours immediately bring to mind a pleasant wintry afternoon. You can find out a lot about life in Holland three hundred and fifty years ago too—the clothes people wore and the houses they lived in. What do you think the poles by the well were used for? Details, such as the little old woman in her chair, the gentleman and his lady, and the sinking boat, make this picture one which you can look at over and over again.

The mute of Kampen

The Dutch painter Avercamp was sometimes called 'de stomme von Kampen' (the mute of Kampen) because he was unable to speak. He was a landscape painter who specialized in ice scenes.

Some of the other pictures in this book won't necessarily have the same immediate appeal. Like other art forms (books, plays, films and so on) a picture isn't always meant to please. There are times when the artist has been too busy putting his thoughts into paint to care how people will react to his pictures. As you turn the pages, try to imagine what response the artist was hoping for.

6

Hendrik Avercamp (1585–1634), *A Scene on the Ice near a Town*. About 1610. 22¾ × 35⅜ in. London, National Gallery.

The Artist

Vincent van Gogh (1853–1890), *Self-portrait at the Easel.* 1888. 25½ × 20 in. Amsterdam, Vincent van Gogh Museum.

You can find out a lot about the way an artist sees things when you look at his paintings. In fact, he is telling us a lot about himself, whether he wants to or not. When you talk to a friend you both express your opinions about things; and in the same way, an artist can't help expressing an opinion about something when he paints it.

Vincent van Gogh (1853–1890)

The Dutch painter Vincent van Gogh was an acutely lonely person, and wrote long letters to his brother Theo about his life and his paintings. He illustrated the letters with little sketches to help Theo share exactly what he was thinking. And in his paintings we are made to share his intense view of the world, to see it as he saw it, and to listen to him when others wouldn't. The five pictures on this and the following page all tell us something about Vincent and his life as a painter.

Van Gogh painted a lot of portraits of other people, but he also painted several of himself. In his painting on the left, he shows how he worked—what he wore, his palette and brushes. This was painted from his reflection in the mirror, so that the picture we can't see is the same as the one here—or is it?

Very soon after painting the portrait on the left Vincent moved from Paris to Arles in the south of France, where, in October 1888, his friend Paul Gauguin visited him. Although they were both artists, they were not alike in other ways. One night they had an argument which upset Vincent terribly. In a frenzy of misery he attacked himself and cut off a piece of his left ear with a razor. Gauguin left Arles straight away and Vincent was taken to hospital. He painted the portrait below while he was convalescing.

Vincent cut off his *left* ear, but in this picture his *right* ear is bandaged. And yet the Japanese print in the background is the right way round! Like all his self-portraits, Vincent painted this one from his reflection in the mirror. But he was particularly fond of the Japanese print, and there was no need to paint that in the mirror—so he copied it as it was.

Vincent van Gogh, *Self-portrait with Bandaged Ear.* 1889. 20 × 17¾ in. London, Courtauld Institute Galleries.

Vincent van Gogh, *The Artist Setting Off for Work.* 1888. 19 × 17¼ in. Formerly Magdeburg, Kaiser-Friedrich Museum.

Another self-portrait?

This isn't exactly a self-portrait, but can you see what it has in common with the first one? It's another painting where the artist shows himself 'in action'—which is a strange idea if you think about it, painting a picture of yourself setting off to paint a picture!

Vincent van Gogh (1853–1890), *Vincent's House in Arles* (detail). 1888. Amsterdam, Vincent van Gogh Museum.

The yellow house

Vincent's house was the one with the green shutters. He painted this picture just after he moved in. You can see why it was called the yellow house! Almost everything here is yellow apart from the deep-blue sky. It looks as if the sunshine which Vincent loved has coloured all the buildings. At the time he was feeling confident that things would work out for him in Arles, and the confidence shows in the cheerful way he has painted this sunny picture.

A place to rest

Vincent sent a sketch of his bedroom to his brother Theo with a description of the painting. It is interesting for us to see what an artist's bedroom was like, almost a hundred years ago, but here Vincent was trying to give a *feeling* of restfulness—as well as just showing how his bedroom looked.

Vincent's own description of the picture

Vincent described the picture to his brother Theo. 'This time it's just simply my bedroom, only here the colour is to do everything, and giving by its simplicity a grander style to things, is to be suggestive here of *rest* or sleep in general. In a word, to look at the picture ought to rest the brain or rather the imagination.'

Vincent van Gogh, *Vincent's Bedroom in Arles*. 1888.
$28\frac{1}{4} \times 35\frac{1}{2}$ in. Amsterdam, Vincent van Gogh Museum.

No rest for Vincent

As things turned out, Vincent didn't get much 'rest' in his life. He continued to throw fits like the one when he cut off his ear, and spent the next two years in the care of doctors, before he eventually committed suicide. But in between fits he painted away furiously. You might come across a famous painting of his called *Wheatfield with Cypresses*. It has none of the peace of the *Bedroom* but is typical of the pictures he painted as his mind became increasingly disturbed.

Animals

Men have painted animals since they've painted pictures—though not always because they liked them. Cave-paintings of animals came from hunters, but the relationship between the painter and his subject hasn't always been between the hunter and the hunted. Painters have been frightened, fascinated or fond of their subjects throughout the history of animal painting. How do you think the painter felt about the animals in each of these pictures?

These greyhounds were built for speed, and in the picture they don't look a bit fierce. Their owner, Lord Grenville, used them for racing and hunting, but they were his pets as well.

The four sketches of cats on the left of the picture opposite look as if Leonardo has drawn his cat from life, and you can see the different shapes a cat makes when he is almost asleep, when he is listening for something, blissfully dreaming or alert and playful. Leonardo, who was also an inventor, was fascinated by the way things worked, including bodies. These sketches were probably for a study about animals in motion.

Body language

Do you think the other cats were drawn from life? They don't look as convincing as the larger ones—their ears are more like a wild cat's. But in these sketches it seems that Leonardo is concentrating even harder on showing the shapes cats make—this time when they are wide awake and fighting. He seems particularly interested in their tails and the way they curl.

The odd one out

There is an animal on this page which is definitely not a cat (can you see it?)! This hissing dragon is curved into a very decorative shape. Perhaps, because there is no such thing as a dragon, Leonardo was using his knowledge of a fighting cat's body to make his mythical dragon look like a real ferocious animal.

ABOVE James Ward (1769–1859), *Three Studies of a Hound* (*Lord Grenville's Greyhound*). 12¾ × 8⅝ in. London, Courtauld Institute of Art.

RIGHT Leonardo da Vinci (1452–1519), *Sketches of Cats*. About 1513. 10⅝ × 8¼ in. London, Royal Collection.

Art from the East

Apart from this one, the only other Japanese print in this book appears in Van Gogh's *Self-portrait with a Bandaged Ear* (p. 8). Western artists have often admired and collected Japanese prints, but art from the east (countries like India, China, Japan) has quite a different history from theirs.

A moral tale

'Every picture tells a story', and this one has a particular moral tale to tell (Kuniyoshi used moral tales from China for several of his pictures). The young man, Tai Shun, had a very hard life. His family was cruel to him and he had the impossible task of making things grow in the barren soil of the

mountains. You can see him scratching away with a wooden rake here. Despite the hardship Tai Shun remained loyal to his family and his work. The birds and the elephants were so impressed by his perseverance that they came to help him out. It's difficult to see exactly *how* they're helping, but Tai Shun has nothing to fear from the huge beasts and swooping birds— they all seem to get along together. Perhaps you can work out what they're doing. The story has a happy ending. The fame of Tai Shun's virtue spread and he was rewarded for his trials by being chosen to marry the Emperor's daughter. Later he became Emperor himself.

Can you see the Japanese writing (called calligraphy) in each of the corners? In the top half of the picture is the story of Tai Shun and a note about the series; in the bottom half is the artist's name (on the left) and his 'hallmark'.

Utagawa Kuniyoshi (1797–1861), *Tai Shun and the Elephants*. 1840. 9½ × 14¼ in. Private collection.

LEFT Albrecht
Dürer (1471–1528),
Sketches of Animals.
1521. $10\frac{1}{2} \times 15\frac{5}{8}$ in.
Williamstown,
Mass., Sterling and
Francine Clark Art
Collection.

RIGHT Jacques-
Laurent Agasse
(1780–1849), *The
Nubian Giraffe.*
1827. $50\frac{1}{8} \times 40$ in.
London, Royal
Collection.

The great German artist Dürer lived almost five
hundred years ago. His drawings from nature
are nearly always extremely detailed and accurate. These sketches show a lioness, a lion, a
baboon and a chamois (a kind of wild goat).

A long way from home

This giraffe looks as out of place amongst the
cattle in the English countryside as his exotic
Sudanese (Nubian) keepers do next to the man
in the top hat. Agasse's painting is of a real
giraffe which was captured in the Sudan and
brought to the royal zoo at Windsor. Unfortunately the giraffe never quite recovered from his
journey and died when four years old.

George Stubbs (1724–1806), *Mares by an Oak Tree.* 1764–5. 39 × 74 in. Ascott, Wing, The National Trust (Rothschild Collection).

Underneath the skin

George Stubbs was a British artist who knew all about horses. He painted 'portraits' of them for their owners. He was also interested in anatomy and spent several months dissecting carcasses of horses to find out just how their muscles moved. (Leonardo was another artist who taught himself anatomy in this way.)

Five mares

You can almost imagine this painting as part of a continuous frieze. The five mares—their colours and shapes—make a decorative pattern against the background of English trees.

Albrecht Dürer (1471–1528), *Study of a Hare* (detail). 1502. 9⅞×9 in. Vienna, Albertina.

It's not difficult to understand why this is one of the best-loved animal pictures. You can almost stroke the fur and the soft ears of this shy creature, and feel his whiskers quivering. Dürer was intensely curious about animals. He kept his own animals and would travel a long way to see an unusual one. In fact, one of these trips was the cause of his death. He caught a fever after a long expedition to the swamps of Zeeland (in Holland) to see a stranded whale.

Gerard Ter Borch (1617–1681), *A Boy Ridding his Dog of Fleas*. 1653–5. 13⅜ × 10⅝ in. Munich, Bayerische Staatsgemäldesammlungen.

Home truths

In the hands of a Dutch painter this picture becomes far more beautiful than you might expect from the title! Seventeenth-century Dutch painters like Ter Borch and Jan Steen (see p. 30) made ordinary home life the subject of their pictures. The attention they gave to light and detail transformed everyday objects into things of rare beauty. The dog seems to understand that his devoted master is doing this for his own good—that expression of long-suffering patience brings the picture immediately to life.

Technicolour baboon

Mandrills are those baboons with blue bottoms and red noses. The Austrian artist Kokoschka painted this one in London Zoo in 1926. At night, in the monkey house, he painted the mandrill and the mandrill glowered back. Kokoschka was quite sure the mandrill detested him (even though he never failed to take the mandrill a banana) but said he saw something of himself in this solitary creature who obviously preferred to be left alone.

A falcon

Holbein was a German artist who painted the famous portraits of Henry VIII and his court which you have probably seen. This painting of a peregrine falcon is absolutely accurate—compare it with a description in a bird book. Such accuracy encourages us to think that his portraits of people were equally true to life.

LEFT Oskar Kokoschka (born 1886), *The Mandrill.* 1926. 50 × 39¾ in. Rotterdam, Boymans-van Beuningen Museum.

RIGHT Hans Holbein (1497/8–1543), *A Falcon* (detail from *Robert Cheseman*). 1533. The Hague, Mauritshuis.

Henri Rousseau

Real or imagined?

Does this fierce tiger frighten you—or does it make you laugh? Do you think the painter actually saw the stormy jungle, or did he imagine it? You can certainly feel the wetness and the tropical warmth.

Le douanier

Rousseau was not a full-time, fully-trained artist but a customs officer ('douanier' in French). Although an amateur, he felt quite sure that he was a great artist. He tried to impress people by saying that his pictures showed scenes he'd witnessed as a soldier in Mexico. For most of his life other artists in Paris were more interested in the work of the Impressionists (such as Monet, Degas, Cézanne, Renoir and others) than in his rather naive and childish paintings. But he was eventually recognised, by Picasso amongst others, and naive painting became highly popular.

Photographic evidence

Many years later a book of photographs of wild animals was discovered to be the source of Rousseau's paintings. He hadn't even been to Mexico! But his lions and tigers were real enough to him. It's said that sometimes he was so frightened by the creatures in his own paintings that he had to go to his studio window to make sure that he wasn't surrounded by the jungle.

Henri Rousseau (1844–1910), *Tropical Storm with a Tiger* (detail). 1891. $51\frac{1}{8} \times 63\frac{3}{4}$ in. London, National Gallery.

Dreams

Alice in Fairyland

This picture might remind you of a story which was being written at about the same time—*Alice in Wonderland*, by Lewis Carroll. It has the same dream-like atmosphere—which is also threatening. What seemed to be a leaf or a twig suddenly turns into a face or an insect. (Look hard at the middle of the picture and you'll see an old man under a wide-brimmed hat.) Do you find you lose your sense of scale amongst the inhabitants of this moonlit world?

The master-stroke

The fairy feller (woodman) is at the bottom of the picture with his back to us and his stone axe raised. His master-stroke will be to split the hazelnut with one blow which will release all the people in the picture from a magic spell. All the fairies have gathered to watch and react to the suspense in different ways. The tall girls on the left are more interested in their own reflections, but the little man at the front seems to have gone cross-eyed with concentration!

Richard Dadd

Richard Dadd spent half his life in a prison mental hospital, but as a young man he was a successful student at the Royal Academy. In 1842 he went off to Egypt to make drawings for a man called Thomas Phillips. While he was abroad he had sunstroke, which seemed to trigger off a mental illness. In August 1843 he murdered his father, was found to be insane and was imprisoned in the Criminal Lunatic Department of the Bethlem Hospital (Bedlam) in London. Fortunately for us, he was provided with brushes and paints so that he could carry on painting for the rest of his life.

Keep on looking

You can look at this picture for hours. Strange creatures of all sizes are hidden amongst the leaves and flowers—there's always one you missed before. The man with the pestle and mortar in the top right-hand corner is Richard Dadd himself.

Richard Dadd (1817–1886). *The Fairy Feller's Master-Stroke* (detail). About 1855–64. London, Tate Gallery.

Photographic effects

Andrew Wyeth is a modern American artist. Modern painters have been born into the age of photography and know the effects it can and can't achieve. In some ways this painting is as realistic as a photograph, but it portrays an idea, or a dream, which a camera can't. One way in which a camera can lie is in the angle the picture is taken from (for example, photographing a low building from low down to make it seem taller). In this painting a sort of 'low-angle' device is used to make the distance between Christina and her home seem greater.

A limited world

Wyeth's neighbour, Christina, had been crippled by polio. A small problem for more able people was a huge challenge for her, and overcoming it a great feat of strength and courage. In this popular painting, Wyeth wanted to show that, because of her courage, Christina's world was not as small or as limited as it must have seemed to those who didn't know her.

Andrew Wyeth (born 1917), *Christina's World*. 1948. $32\frac{1}{4} \times 47\frac{3}{4}$ in. New York, Museum of Modern Art.

Jan Steen (1625/6–1679), *The Village School*. 1670. 33 × 43 in. Edinburgh, National Gallery of Scotland (on loan from the Duke of Sutherland).

At School

What sort of school is this?

There's a lot going on in this picture, but very little of it has to do with learning! One teacher is so busy helping two of the children that she's ignoring the rest of the class, and the other seems to have given up trying to keep order altogether. The chaotic classroom looks more like a barn.

Dutch schoolchildren 300 years ago

Although the village school itself is probably not typical, you can get a good idea of the way children dressed three hundred years ago; you can see their books and other equipment, including their lunch baskets, in this painting. The Dutch artist has painted every detail.

Jan Steen painted a lot of comic scenes like this one, often giving a topsy-turvy view of everyday life. In fact, in Holland, the phrase 'a Jan Steen household' means one where everything is disorganised!

Rembrandt's only son

Titus was thirteen when his father, the great Dutch artist Rembrandt, made this portrait of him sketching. Rembrandt and his wife Saskia had four children but Titus was the only one who didn't die as a baby. Poor Saskia herself died soon after Titus was born, and he was brought up by a kindly woman called Hendrickje Stoffels. Rembrandt painted a large number of portraits, especially self-portraits. He often used his family as models for bigger pictures as well. Titus appears in these sometimes as the young Joseph (who had the coat of many colours), and as the boy Jesus, and as many other characters from Bible stories. Titus died before his father, when he was only twenty-seven.

Rembrandt van Rijn (1606–1669), *Portrait of Titus* (detail). 1665. $30\frac{1}{4} \times 24\frac{3}{4}$ in. Rotterdam, Boymans-van Beuningen Museum.

At Home

What's going on?

Five hundred years ago, when there were no cameras to take photographs of a special occasion, a rich family might have hired an artist to do the job. This picture of an Italian businessman, Giovanni Arnolfini, and his wife Giovanna could be a type of fifteenth-century 'wedding photograph'. There are plenty of clues to show us that there is something special going on. The room is very quiet (they've taken off their shoes) and Giovanni's raised hand seems to ask for silence. Also the couple are wearing their best clothes, which look as if they are rather hot for the time of year (can you see the tree with ripe cherries on it outside the window?).

More clues

People living at the same time as the Arnolfinis would have found more clues in this picture. For example, the faithful little griffin terrier meant that Giovanni and Giovanna should be true to one another. And although Giovanna is not pregnant (that was just the shape artists gave to women at the time), there is a little carving of St Margaret, patron saint of child-birth, on the bedpost.

The Arnolfinis at home

The Arnolfinis are pictured in a bedroom (probably not the one they slept in) in their large city house. All the furniture is expensive and well-made. You can see the intricate work in the rug, the chandelier and the mirror. Even the oranges tell us something—they were probably very expensive and difficult to buy in a country where they didn't grow.

The artist

Jan van Eyck was an important citizen of Bruges (in the part of Flanders which is now Belgium). Quite apart from the fame he and his older brother Hubert shared as painters, Jan was well-respected for his work as a diplomat and politician. Jan was one of the first artists to experiment with oil paints and in this picture he has taken delight in using the special shiny qualities of oil paint to show how the summer light from the open window strikes the different textures in the dark and quiet room (the candle was only there for telling the time).

Jan van Eyck was here

Who do you think were the witnesses at this wedding? Well, we are—and so was Van Eyck himself. He tells us so with a flourish by signing it: 'Jan van Eyck was here in 1434', and, more subtly, by painting his own reflection in the convex mirror beneath it.

Jan van Eyck (about 1390–1441), *The Arnolfini Marriage*. 1434. $32\frac{1}{4} \times 23\frac{1}{2}$ in. London, National Gallery.

LEFT John Singer Sargent (1856–1925), '*Carnation, Lily, Lily, Rose*' (detail). 1885–6. 68½ × 60½ in. London, Tate Gallery.

RIGHT Pierre-Auguste Renoir (1856–1919), *At the Piano* (detail). 1892. 45⅝ × 35½ in. Paris, Louvre.

Preparing for the party

These two girls have the pleasant task of lighting the candles inside the Chinese lanterns and stringing them up amongst the flowers in the garden. They had to concentrate because the lanterns were made from paper. It looks as if it's going to be a magical party!

Life in a French home

Renoir made everything he painted look happy, and these girls seem to be having great fun playing the piano. The room which you can see in the background gives the impression of a well-ordered French family home, with pictures on the wall and flower-arrangements.

Games

A town full of children

This painting looks very much like a modern school playground, but in fact there is no school in sight and the scene is set in a Dutch or Flemish town of four hundred years ago. And when you look closely at the children's faces, do they still look like children? Or are they miniature adults?

Eighty different games

But whether they are real or not, the children in this picture are playing real and recognisable games. You have probably spotted some of them already—swimming, playing with dolls, stilts, spinning tops, a swing, hide-and-seek, leapfrog—as as well as climbing and fighting. Can you see some children playing an old-fashioned game of jacks? It explains why some people still call it knucklebones. There are plenty more games for you to identify, although you'll have to guess at some of them.

Balloons and waterwings

Have you ever wondered what balloons and other toys were made of before plastic or rubber were discovered? The boy learning to swim in this picture has water-wings made from inflated pigs' bladders (which is what balloons were made from). See if you can work out from this picture what these toys used to be made from: hoops, climbing frame, skittles, marbles and bowls.

Pieter Bruegel (1525/30–1569), *Children's Games* (detail). 1560. 46½ × 63⅜ in. Vienna, Kunsthistorisches Museum.

Georges de la Tour (1593–1652), *The Cheat with the Ace of Diamonds* (detail). About 1625–9. 102 × 123½ in. Paris, Landry Collection.

More than one cheat?

There's a lot of cheating going on here—and you're easily had if you think that the detail on the right comes from the painting on this page! In fact, it comes from another very similar picture where the cards had been shuffled differently. The cheat with the ace of diamonds on the left and the other shady characters in bright clothing are hoodwinking the rich boy on the right into gambling his gold away. And it looks as if they are succeeding!

Candlelight

The drama of this picture is heightened by the lighting. Many of the artists in this book have paid great attention to the way daylight falls on different textures. Georges de la Tour was fascinated by the light and shadow cast by candles (two hundred and fifty years before the invention of the electric light bulb). Here the light brings out the glint in the central courtesan's eyes, the sheen of the rich boy's embroidered shirt and the gleam of the gold.

40

Georges de la Tour, *The Cheat with the Ace of Clubs* (detail). About 1625. Geneva, Marier Collection.

Mean old man

The brilliance of La Tour's work was only rediscovered very recently. He and his family lived in a small French town, Lunéville, far from any city which was a centre for artistic ideas. Unfortunately, the town records of Lunéville show that this wonderful artist was not a popular character. He was fined for letting rubbish pile up outside his house, kept a large number of unruly dogs and was mean with his money.

Into Battle!

The battle of Waterloo

June 18th, 1815, the day Napoleon took on the British army at Waterloo, wasn't very romantic for the soldiers who were fighting. But because Napoleon was defeated, ending many years of wars with France, it became a glorious day in the minds of the British people, celebrated long afterwards in poems and paintings.

Getting it right

Lady Elizabeth Butler painted *Scotland for Ever* sixty-six years later. It shows the Scots Greys regiment as they charged their French attackers. She was very keen to paint the battle as it actually was, and through her husband, who was a general, she persuaded the commanding officer of the Scots Greys to form up his regiment and charge at her as she sat at her easel. We have to assume that her painting wasn't altogether accurate or she'd have been mown down almost before she started; the horses are galloping faster than they would have done in battle and they're also on a collision course with each other!

What really happened

In fact the Scots Greys lost hundreds of men and horses at Waterloo. For several days they had neither slept properly nor eaten, and were so wet the night before the battle that the colour from their red coats ran into their white belts. Although they drove back the French successfully, many of the Scots Greys chased them too far and were killed by enemy lancers.

Elizabeth Butler (1846–1933), *Scotland for Ever* (detail). 1881. 40 × 76 in. Leeds, City Art Gallery.

Paolo Uccello (1397–1475), *St George and the Dragon*. About 1460. 22¼ × 29¼ in. London, National Gallery.

The age of chivalry

The real St George was a Roman soldier, born and martyred in Palestine, but we know him as the chivalrous horseman of the Middle Ages, the original knight in shining armour. You'd be right in imagining that there's been some confusion! Crusaders visited St George's shrine (he was killed for refusing to persecute the Christians) at a place called Lydda. Now Lydda was also the place where Perseus (in the Greek myth) was supposed to have rescued the beautiful Andromeda from the sea monster. So the stories got mixed up. St George, who was also patron saint of Genoa in Italy, was adopted by England only a short time before Uccello painted this picture.

Fifteenth-century fashions

Paolo Uccello was an Italian artist who lived in Florence more than five hundred years ago. This painting is one of the oldest canvases (there are older paintings in books, on wood, and on walls) to survive. The princess's hairstyle and dress, quite the height of fashion in the 1460s, gave clues to the date of the painting.

Two-legged dragon

Part of the fun of painting a dragon is that you can let your imagination run riot. You can make it a bird or a reptile, a dinosaur or the end-result of 'heads, bodies and legs'. (On p. 13 Leonardo was experimenting with dragon shapes.) Uccello's dragon has wings and two legs like a bird, teeth and claws like a wild beast, and a scaly reptilian tail—but somehow he doesn't look very fierce. Do you find yourself feeling just a bit sorry for him?

OPPOSITE Philip James de Loutherbourg (1740–1812), *The Shipwreck* (detail). 1793. Southampton Art Gallery.

ABOVE Francisco de Goya (1746–1828), *The Colossus*. About 1812. $45\frac{1}{2} \times 41\frac{1}{2}$ in. Madrid, Prado.

Pirates!

Travelling by sea is safer these days, when lifeboats and helicopters can come and rescue you. But two hundred years ago sea travellers really were in danger from pirates and thieves, who were out to rob passengers of the worldly goods they travelled with. Many ships were lured onto the rocks by wreckers, who then looted the cargo and slew the passengers.

Giant of war

Goya was a Spanish painter who was deeply moved by the troubles besetting his country during the Napoleonic Wars at the beginning of the nineteenth century (for quite a different view of these wars, see p. 43) and his paintings reflected their general feelings of fear and anxiety. This giant symbolises havoc and destruction, striking terror wherever he goes.

Pablo Picasso (1881–1973), *Guernica*. 1937. 138 × 308 in. New York, on loan to the Museum of Modern Art.

The bombing of Guernica

From 1936 to 1939 there was civil war in Picasso's native country, Spain. Picasso, who hated war and violence in any form, was particularly horrified by an incident that took place in April 1937. The Condor Brigade (aircraft belonging to Franco's German allies) flew over the ancient town of Guernica on market day and bombed it (so the story goes) to the ground. Picasso, who lived in France, was spurred into action and began this painting straight away.

A huge project

Guernica is an enormous painting. The canvas measures roughly 3.5 m by 7.5 m (it would fill a whole wall in most rooms). Painting it became something of a public event. Picasso kept the sketches he did beforehand, and people photographed him and talked with him while he worked. The final picture is not easy to understand right away—it contains many of Picasso's personal ideas and symbols. Here are some things to look out for amongst the frightening

distortions which represent the horrors of war: a bull (this stands, very roughly, for brutality); a horse (which stands, again very roughly, for the people who are the victims of brutality); a woman leaning from a window, holding a lamp; a fallen warrior with a broken sword; a weeping woman with a baby in her arms. Look and see if you can find any other images of war.

Picasso and the twentieth century

Picasso died in 1973, and we describe him as a modern artist, but when he was very young he was painting at the same time as Van Gogh, Renoir and Munch! If you compare their paintings (pages 10–13, 35 and 52) you begin to get an idea of just how much Picasso changed the nature of painting. The speed of change in the twentieth century has of course been greater than ever before, so you might expect there to be more drastic changes in the history of its art. What happened at Guernica was very much a twentieth-century incident and Picasso responded in a truly twentieth-century style.

Faces

Something fishy

There's certainly something fishy about this portrait! It comes to life rather differently from most (the only human thing about it is the general shape and the eye). Archimboldo was an Italian portrait painter who lived four hundred years ago. Do you think he was tempted to portray some of his more respectable sitters in the same way? Official court painter in his day, he is now better remembered for these fantastic heads. In others, called *Summer*, *Winter*, and so on, the face was put together from fruits, vegetables and all sorts of everyday objects. Try and identify all the different fish shown here.

Giuseppe Archimboldo (1527–1593), *Water*. 1566.
Vienna, Kunsthistorisches Museum.

Edvard Munch (1863–1944), *The Scream*. 1893. Oslo, Nasjonalgalliert.

Audio-visuals

There aren't many pictures you can hear! But a long and winding wail wraps itself around almost everything in the picture on the left (only the two men walking off down the straight road seem unaware of what's happening). No wonder the despairing figure with the skull-like head is trying to block out the noise.

After van Gogh

The Norwegian artist Munch had some of the same ideas as another artist in this book, Van Gogh (see pages 8–11). He wanted people to *feel* something when they looked at his pictures. Do the feelings of sadness and anxiety expressed in *The Scream* reach you when you look at the picture?

Sad sunset

Munch kept a diary. There is an entry in it describing an evening walk in Oslo (then called Christiana) with two friends. This is what he wrote: 'The sun set. I felt a twinge of melancholy. Suddenly the sky became a bloody red. I stopped and leaned against the railing, dead tired, and I looked at the flaming clouds that hung like blood over the blue-black fjord and the city. My friends walked on. I stood there, trembling with fright. And I felt a loud unending scream piercing nature.' Do you think that the words and the picture express the same feeling?

Fighting faces and grotesque faces

The most famous face Leonardo da Vinci painted belonged to a lady called La Gioconda, otherwise known as the Mona Lisa. Nobody knows for certain her real name. Leonardo was a musician, an engineer, a mathematician, an inventor (he made designs for aeroplanes five hundred years ago) and a well-known horseman, as well as a painter and sculptor. He left very few finished paintings, though there are thousands of sketches and drawings. These two pictures show his curiosity about every sort of human face—not just the pretty ones.

Leonardo da Vinci (1452–1519), *Five Grotesque Heads*. About 1494. $10\frac{1}{4} \times 8\frac{1}{8}$ in. London, Royal Collection.

Leonardo da Vinci (1452–1519), *Portrait of Mona Lisa*. 1503. $30\frac{3}{8} \times 20\frac{7}{8}$ in. Paris, Louvre.

Fashionable London faces

Percy is the white cat (whose face you can't see). Ossie Clark and his wife Celia are both successful clothes designers. Hockney has painted a portrait where you can find out as much about the Clarks from how they have furnished their London home as from their faces.

David Hockney

David Hockney is an English artist from Bradford who now lives in London and Paris. His photographic likenesses are often taken from actual photographs. You might find it interesting to compare this portrait of the Clarks—and their cat— with Van Eyck's one of the Arnolfinis—and their dog— painted more than five hundred years earlier.

David Hockney (born 1937), *Mr and Mrs Clark and Percy*. 1970–1. 84 × 120 in. London, Tate Gallery.

The king of rock'n'roll

This picture shows Elvis Presley at various stages in his extraordinary career. Elvis was the most successful rock 'n' roll singer ever (you can see that Oxtoby has called him 'Mr Rock' in the top left-hand corner), although in the last few years before his death in 1977 he abandoned the wildness that had made him famous. You can trace the progress of Elvis's career through the different portraits of him that make up the complete picture. We see him at the beginning, in 1956, when he made one of his most famous records, '*Don't Be Cruel*'; in 1958, in the film *Jailhouse Rock*; during his service in the U.S. Army; and during the last few years of his life. Can you tell which is which?

The rock'n'roll artist

David Oxtoby was at art college with David Hockney (see pages 54-5 and 62). He was growing up in the 1950s when rock 'n' roll stars such as Elvis, Buddy Holly and Chuck Berry were changing the world of popular music. A great many of his paintings and drawings are of these stars, as well as more recent ones like Paul McCartney and Elton John.

David Oxtoby (born 1938), *Elvis Fan Mag.* 22½ × 15½ in.

OPPOSITE Peter Blake (born 1932), *On the Balcony*. 1955-7. 47¾ × 35¾ in. London, Tate Gallery.

ABOVE Derek Boshier (born 1937), *The Identi-Kit Man*. 1962. 72 × 72 in. London, Tate Gallery.

Pop art

These two paintings are examples of Pop Art. Both artists use familiar objects and images from the mass media (magazines, advertisements and so on) as material for their pictures. See if you can find the royal family on the balcony of Buckingham Palace, and a copy of the play *Romeo and Juliet*. On the far left is a portrait of the artist, reflected in the boy's sunglasses.

The toothpaste man

Is this what you see in your bathroom mirror? Derek Boshier has made up a jigsaw man from the sort of advertisements that influence us all. Clearly the toothpaste man no longer has a mind of his own!

Optical illusions

Does this picture make you feel sea-sick or uncomfortable? If you look at it hard (but not for too long!), you can see the shape of a wave very clearly. After a while the whole picture starts to jump and flicker. Bridget Riley painted a lot of these 'op-art' pictures, most of them in black and white. In *Crest* the same wavy line is reproduced 128 times.

Bridget Riley (born 1931), *Crest*. 1964. $65\frac{3}{8} \times 65\frac{3}{8}$ in. Peter Stuyvesant Foundation.

What's gone wrong?

Hogarth drew this picture to show what might happen if an artist couldn't handle perspective (the method which allows artists to make objects in the distance the right size). Even so, an artist would have to know all about perspective to put these ingenious 'mistakes' into practice! Hogarth was a London artist of the eighteenth century who made very popular engravings illustrating moral tales. They often made fun of well-known characters of his day and had titles like 'The Rake's Progress', 'Beer Street' and 'Gin Lane' and 'Marriage à la Mode'.

William Hogarth (1697–1764), *False Perspective.* 1754.

David Hockney (born 1937), *A Bigger Splash*. 1966–7.
96 × 96 in. Private collection.

Is there anybody there?

This picture teases the brain because it only tells you half the story. There are people in it, but you can't see them. There's movement, but the movement has been suddenly cut short—frozen in time and space by the click of a camera, before there's been time for the ripples to spread or a wet human head to emerge spluttering from the water. Meanwhile, the harsh Californian sun blazes down timelessly on the house and the empty chair and the palm trees. Hockney painted three *Splash* pictures. This is the largest one and the most famous. Its name suggested the title for a film about the artist, which came out in 1975.